FOREVER YOUNG

FOREVER YOUNG

A Sequel 2.0

William Friedman

Library of Congress Control Number:		2019906518
ISBN:	Hardcover	978-1-7960-3819-4
	Softcover	978-1-7960-3818-7
	eBook	978-1-7960-3817-0

Print information available on the last page.

Rev. date: 06/12/2019

To order additional copies of this book, contact:
Xlibris
1-888-795-4274
www.Xlibris.com
Orders@Xlibris.com
788451

To Kristin, my constant love

And Maguy, whose griefs I share

This book is a companion piece to *Youth Lasts Forever. Forever Young: A Sequel 2.0* repeats the device of rhymed stanzas. It is my fourth book of poetry.

First, credit is due to Mrs. Maguy Joseph, whose husband became ill. But really, first is Kristin Weal, my reliable companion for over two decades. Without her, I'd only have a cold statuette like Hermione in *The Winter's Tale*. Her warmth follows me everywhere—a sculpture brought to life.

As for myself, I began my study of literature and love for poetry at Williams College (which, next to Harvard, is surely the best liberal arts school in America).

I was also a teacher at Howard University, the foremost black school in America. My fixation and fascination with black studies began there when I read the James Baldwin companion.

Taken as a whole, he penned
a fiction far ahead of its time.
If mastery failed him,
in many ways he would start all over again.

I'm proud of you, of the lightness
of your footsteps hiding in the stars.
Your choice to entertain
the angels and seraphim in strict file.

Why, in some foreign land
where folks are kind and without wrath,
I dream of a Shangri-la, a paradise
with manna and sweet nectar that would
forever last.

That time you wandered through the town,
led the Pied Piper, children following,
the upraised corpses in their graves
would follow your wide renown.

Lovingly and gently, the players
in Hamlet showed their art
before kings and queens and cowardly friends
all of whom played their part.

One more time before we go,
I awaited this song all week.
A soldier is defaced by the war,

unaware victim whose past death
could hardly creep.

I was serious in my endeavor
to sight the planets.
The stars above gave me light
enough to read a book, having won the fight.

The truth being forced on me—
allegations I'd done no wrong;
I write to the rhythm of the music,
the lyrics and time scheme of the song.

Where did the truth lie,
underneath a mistletoe or "ivy never sere"?
Compelled patience and passion
like a holy writ that could fly.

Given enough space and time,
our love shall shine bright.
Who then am I to question or complain
of the coming and fading of the light?

What's true and what's possible
are two different things.
With more than human life spans,
we'll reunite in heaven as soon as we can.

It seemed possible, in a span of years,
that our two lives might once again
unite; by the high clouds, through the stars,
our mutual dreams probably ending in tears.

I can complain if I feel weak
about the planet's woes.

Tell me what I should do
if I fear facing my earthly foes.

That was it. In the end,
nothing much or special to review.
I tried that summer to learn
about the birds and the butterflies from
their easy slumber too.

By now, I exercise my verbal muscles.
I'm in the middle of a quandary;
should I not propose to you?
Back home, sinners hustle.

I ate heartily at the banquet—
well-braised meat and Maine potatoes.
At the door, the portico, the poor awaited
shreds and bones of which they were capable.

Hail and farewell! Ave atque vale!
Compare the elements of future times.
Will I feel the vestiges of the present
even as the past shows a newer event?

I was lost along the trail.
Weary were my legs and bones.
Did I leave her to the danger of bears and lions?
Hibernation in winter left me,
a hunter, all alone.

She grew impatient, that I knew.
My pen, like greased lightning,
traveled afar with India ink,
never for a single moment relaxing, dying, or defying.

I took a sidelong glance
at her long hair. I admired in the
mirror her tall frame.
Did she appeal to me?
Or was I in fantasy totally sharing?

What if I dither, if I waste time?
Anxious to get back to you,
I proudly recall images of childhood
we both shared living in the hood.

I waste time that I should take seriously,
like a gospel hymn in a Protestant church;
when would this boredom disappear,
like Sunday service of no real worth?

Did it matter either way
I tried to defend the truth?
As I went along a dusty road,
I watched the beauteous magic that
she displayed, a mere youth.

There must have been some
explanation
(other than those that came simply).
Instead of working my fingers to the
bone,
I sought companionship rather than
remain alone.

Alone in a field of clover
or lavender in the south of France,
grape pickers tired their backs
in the midst of nature, their lean
bodies relaxed.

Must I remember those days
when I had to function on my own?
Sweet how those memories were to
tempt me to revisit my passions long
gone.

I told you so—or so I thought.
I place pretty music on the stereo;
hardly, never alone,
avant-garde tunes exquisitely
wrought.

I left it all up to you,
that time we gathered in Faneuil Hall.
As rebels, we stood our ground;
as patriots, we neither sought any
renown.

I visited all the churches in Paris—
in Gothic or Angevin style.
They gave me such peace of mind
that I lingered in each of them awhile.

Circumstances had put me in a sour mood.
How could I level the playing field,
get back to my usual thinking self,
a Homo sapiens returning to what is
real and can heal what is good?

I had a glimpse of Maine's rocky shore,
the water too cold surely in winter.
I was aware of the ice you could drive a
truck over
by cypresses and pines on which the
snow did linger.

"Take a chance," the barker said
in his booming baritone voice.
To shoot duck decoys all in a row,
I lost ten dollars in the game of chance, of choice.

O for a taste, an elixir
of that special brew!
Cassandra might take it as a bad sign,
like the dropping of another shoe.

Was I prepared, in case it rained,
to embark on a voyage to Cythera?
Fancy folk in manners baroque
Watteau and Fragonard in rococo
refrain.

I set my sights on Monday,
on a site out in the southwest.
At the Alamo, patriots made a last stand.
They died bravely against forces
they couldn't withstand.

Time and time again, I argued
with that professor who was always right.
I took my time and was patient,
like a flock of egrets taking flight.

So I surprised myself. In swift retort,
I remark to myself a fresh sound;
the wind blew heavenly from the west.
I gave up hopes of any renown.

So I went deeper into that *tulgy wood* (Jabberwocky),
unafraid in daylight of scary beasts.
The roots of bamboo trees
I skirted as best I could.

Calypso song by Harry Belafonte,
who later advocated for civil rights.
On the mainland where slavery
flourished,
he was born with his race proudly to fight.

On the cave walls were where Giotto
created his frescoes
of sacred men and angelic figures
that existed for him since time began
as he had lingered or had figured.

As the end of the day approached,
dusk arriving early,
skylarks built their nests in the bushes
to enjoy in peace their humble
existence nearby.

Imagine walking the cobblestones to
the Tower of London.
Blake saw the shining city
where unhappy souls walked the plank,
where the Queen's royal jewels filled in
the colors that heretofore had been
left blank.

I began at the beginning, when I saw
success stalking and starting to be achieved;
our country clearing, cleaning up its act,
fulfilled the high hopes it received.

Both of us felt chipper
as the sun rose amid starry clouds.
Rather than be tricked by the weather,
I, a sole trooper, would avoid the
lonely crowd.

Without religion, John Lennon imagined,
we wouldn't all go to the devil.
Not to fear, faith and charity,
next to love and hate, would suffer
quite little.

And each flower at each hedgerow's end
like a balloon fills the air.
It's all been said since time began
or immemorial:
flocks of birds and schools of
fish stick together and share.

And still, stabs of woe color my memory.
I want to let it all out.
About children inheriting a sad world
as aloof as a Sherlock Holmes mystery.

Nature's history left far behind,
I can say only so much about it.
Sphinxes and pyramids withstand
eons of decay, multitudes of sand.

Do I like you? Love you?
You know darn well
today ain't the time
when mountains crumble to sand
in meadows of dew.

As I continue on down the road,
ant holes and beehives arise
in the dewy dawn of summer
and the animals in nature win the prize.

If I am far from perfect,
who else will know?
A muse draws circles around me,
around these same figures as the sleet
and snow.

If I write an epic poem as
old as Homer or as new as Milton and
Wordsworth,
will I allow myself enough space
to match the ancients with the
moderns right here on earth?

So who cares if my afternoon
fled by too fast, like a butterfly
or tiger lily left out in the elements
in spring when rebirth has just begun?

I owed everything to her,
although my pockets were empty.
How to make her see clearly
the conundrum my heart was set in?

We hung together at the dance.
All together we would go
around the purple heather
in spring, hearts that sought romance slow.

As we carried on, our marching band
took the field. Like the players
on both teams, a level playing field
of sports, we weren't the best of
soothsayers.

An effort was made by me that hour
long after my injuries were on the mend.
The sport had kept us on the field
long after those efforts I did intend.

Once again, yon yew tree,
yon green laurels.
I, a king, had my crown and scepter,
which I'd employ to the twelfth of never.

How could I live without her?
Without her wiles, her sweet
protestations?
Then she asked me to accompany her
to a secret tryst, away from common
relations.

I could go on, continue forever.
Riddles of the universe possessed my mind.
Maybe I wasn't doing as good as usual
as I sought the Holy Grail, the only
treasure I could find.

She "possessed me merely" (Hamlet).
I set up a soliloquy out in the sun.
What egress was I seeking
to find love so meekly?

The saw drilled down on the wood.
Lumberjacks cut logs for the river.
In Maine, they filled the long lakes,
the habitat more hospitable than ever.

I talked back to the teacher.
I had used a vocabulary unclear,

even uncouth.
Did he seek me out as an opponent
of the truth? An untrustworthy youth?

Moving down the highway,
take it to the limit.
The hitchhiker hailed a car
from Boston westward that would take
him afar, and but in a minute.

"Early one morning," Dylan Thomas
wrote,
awoken in a sleepy village in Wales,
country imagined in greenish color
with little harbors opening their sails.

I kept on dreaming of women
who were paragons of virtue—
not delayed or rushed
but careful in that they observed a
curfew.

I only went so far,
blessing the climate of foreign lands.
Blood dripped from long swords,
only soiling the dirt with filthy hands.

What was the mystery
that encircled our impending days?
I sought no escape from modern inventions,
only challenging my soul to grave conventions.

My spirit spoke to my soul.
In any situation, I was having fun.
I directed passionate words
to the recipient woman who surely was
the one.

How could I resist her wiles
when so much present fortune was at
stake going on?
Happiness sought me in unsuspected places, spaces.
I stepped up to the line feeling
cheerier, feeling chipper all the while.

How do you figure? Those fears
unrelenting, precarious in wartime;
how could I avoid—in safe passage—
the false rainbow I only knew to be mine?

I acquired two poetry anthologies at the bookstore
where there were quite a few new ones.
Why do I study all this other verse
when mine are better!—don't jump the gun.

Scholarship surrounds us
in this bookstore café.
Lest I feel overwhelmed,
I focus on my personal worth and
worldly wealth today.

The batter was ruled out by the umpire:
"Three strikes and you're out."
The ballplayers had steak for
breakfast. With loaded stomachs,
they gave the team from Brooklyn a loud shout.

Unfortunately, his mind was twisted.
In socializing, he feared all society.
With the promise of improvement,
all sorts of knowledge remained a
mystery.

He carved out a place on Mount
Rushmore
in the middle of the midwestern desert.
Hurrying back to his workshop,
to his model sculpture, he felt pride
when he rested.
She served me with food,
staples necessary to be eaten.
Whether coffee, tea, or a cool drink,
the headmaster
blessed me; and I avoided a
beating.

The pleasant beverage on my table
would bring joy on such a cool day.
I started to smile at my felicity,
my facility to accept a gift relayed.

What a quandary! A conundrum!
Poets from around the world snickered,
but I applied my genius as a prodigy
to geometric sums and totals already
figured.

When the sky fell (feared Chicken Little),
the angels flew to a safer place.
With "ease in their bearing,"
they took it as an occasion to save face.
I had done enough that fortnight.
I tried hard to be individual.
Before a bank, I dreamed of being a millionaire;
by the brook, a tadpole or a minnow
as per usual.

"That's an idea," she wrote.
Mary, Mary, quite contrary.
How does your garden grow?
Where would lessons at school end?
Like deep-sea diver fearful of the
bends.
I don't do more than one thing at a time,
marvels surely passed out of my head.
Try doing two or more things at once
leads to failure, an awkward place I'd
find. I'd dread.

I traveled down the line
to the place where Lucy dwelled;
trying to avoid other poets' styles,
I comported myself right or well.

Something made me rush
to places where I felt secure.
Like an amateur poet,
I only rarely tried to knock on another door.

Cherokee woman, salt of the earth,
whose simple grace assaults the hours.
Once, for a while, I pause, I slow down,
your mystery like a cool April shower.

To conclude, as I began,
where nothing stand in my way
to imagine someone dreaming,
drowning—imagine!—on such a
glorious day.

Late for the meeting,
for my month's work, actually,

I followed, like a mystic, evil hours
when I had no inclination for
dreaming.

Imagine, dream of a Holy Grail,
a holy week's pilgrimage to Mecca
or Mussina, where observers unite
before Mohammed, asserting their rights.

What are human rights?
In law, the promise of due process!
When we deprive people of their rights,
justice won't permit its allowance.

My allowance in high school was fair.
The sun shone dreamily on my head;
Stephen Daedalus's potted meat
an ideal provision, fair and square.

This time, I swear I'll quit;
I was in the neighborhood of King
Kublai Khan.
Dictators, strongmen since time began,
Trump tops them all, faulting
God's plan.
I rested at a pit stop
on my way—my way or the highway!
Drivers and truckers didn't hamper me;
I understood what my overall fate would be.

My willpower, my desire to succeed,
I meant only to impress my love.
As time goes by, I traveled
a thousand miles to return her glove.

Was something left out?
I could easily see
what no postmortems
meant to me.

I took a break.
Lest time would stand still,
I obeyed her every command
where fortune and luck might lend a
hand.

The effort was worthwhile.
I was to advocate for causes—
if Al-Qaeda or ISIS ruled the caliphate,
still I'd lie in the sun and try to smile.

I swore to uphold the king's values,
to act spiritually in terms of the
church and the law.
Barely beyond in years,
my troubles lodged from a hawk's perch.

I wonder why she was so good to me.
What did I do to merit such service?
Such servitude? Certitude reigned supreme:
in the grand sum of things, unity not reversed.

I threw a Hail Mary pass.
My intrepid receiver caught it.
In sports, I only moderately excelled;
in running only was I unsurpassed, alas!

The cave by the sea's roar
was handy for Cymbeline. A shelter
where water and spume ne'er reached us
in a fantasy once where I resided
before.

———

It impressed me: her locks, her eyes,
her grace, natural under the sun
where all my restive urges reside
from the start, able to hold back the
tide.

What did I lack, that temperate winter?
When snow melted and ice wasn't a menace?
What did I need to fulfill my urges
when weddings swiftly defeated
funeral dirges?

I understand fully what you meant.
It seemed like such a waste.
Oxen pulled a plough through the fallow land
and carved ruts where seedlings remain.

It still wasn't time to stop.
And I knew it was hopeless—
like the hapless youth who
was caught by a tightrope or yoke.

The best always came at the end.
Phony money not needed at all.
I worked my fingers to the bone.
After all this work, I'm hardly alone.

Maybe you amaze me
with your tears and with your smiles.
No, I didn't forget your presence,
two lucky lovers alone for a while.

And what was the question you phrased?
(I use a better pen.)
We sat by a sunny window.

Our objective: to avoid the latest craze.
If left alone, I can pursue
the vibrations starting in my heart.
With no access verbiage,
two lovers hardly kept apart.

The color of the sun was blocked
as we sat inside watching it.
Black and white kids, like in a dream,
yielded obstacles between them,
hard as a rock.

Did I bore her to death?
Selfishly I persisted.
Prepared for any unsought
circumstances.
Being with her took away all my
breath, my senses.

Slowly the subway came into the
station.
She allowed me time to prepare;
she called me in advance.
I was the recipient of her slightest glance.

What is this message I send,
to juries of the innocent,
to proposals of the law court,
of emotions I must vent?

Such continuity was necessary.
I write when my spirit moves me.
Two countries in the Balkans,
would certain wars consume me?

Hold me tight.
Never let me go.
In Afghanistan where I was born,
I return to where I began.

You inspire me like a judge
who can assess my worth
not in reverse but in regard
to the soft fineries of the sod, of the earth.

She's impatient.
I'm tied to the present
like a bird, a canary, in a coal mine.
Tell me. You're always on my mind.

With fresh relish, I wish I weren't so
blind. Incorrigible the bully. Attuned my heart.
As music drowns me in ecstasy,
I make the effort to save my soul,
fully open to play in my regarded
memory.

As age consumes me year by year
and as my birthday comes in a
month,
choirs of angelic singers in Bavaria
force and send me to the battle's front.

Eerily night birds, blindly
like a nocturnal owl
with funny, beady eyes,
sing me asleep before I even try.

In fifteen minutes, the microwave
will warm my leftover pasta.

In the meantime, I read the *Times,*
taking care not to spill sauce on my
newspaper.

The time was precious; the time was precarious.
In progress, I couldn't rush
or be forced to think only of you
on a safari in the African bush.

It must have been urgent,
when you looked down on me.
I appreciate your frankness, your squalor,
like love and truth forced upon me.

Knock on wood, I tapped my knuckles
on the cold surface of my desk.
That was where I worked the hardest,
denying mistakes of fabrics damask.

Quickly I hurried.
We had plans to fill that morn
besides buying groceries and
shopping for articles.
Early we started at dawn.

Concentrate on the page.
Make remarks between the white lines.
With shreds of comments,
I seek any quality of life I can find.

Again, Kristin sits while I write
in code, in allegory, in metaphor.
I challenge myself above present troubles;
don't imagine I do any of these things out of spite.

"Respectfully, Will." I finished a letter.
But not to my nemesis the devil.
At the Académie française, teachers
invoke the fine arts as they are able.

To where does my mind wander?
To forests and woods where mushrooms grow,
to sunken frigates in the sea,
to unknown fantasies that follow me.

If, in some way, I can help,
make you "see with my eyes,"
stand in my shoes,
prevent you from taking more abuse,
accepting any more lies.

In the city, the houses
painted pink and split-level
were suggestive of any joys.
We in Hyde Park from our nap were
aroused.

She must have been somebody's baby;
her qualities were beyond reproach.
I search everywhere for an explanation,
but it showed only in orange
marmalade eaten
with toast.

What was the reason? The
implication
behind the thorny branches that clung
on to the wall? To suffer too much sun
or drown in gutter water, spoiling the
berries among.

If you took me seriously,
why didn't I see it from the first?
The implements I use to execute the
truth
used by cavemen ready to rehearse?

All around town, it was loudly said
that you honored me from the first.
Pronounced in church and cemetery,
where our bodies eventually would be
laid to rest.

Hold on to the reins. The palomino
bucked as I rode her white belly.
In the hot prairie, a two-mile hike
for both the two of us would be merry.

What was the object of her objections?
The reason for playing hooky at school?
Rare were the studious fellows
who learned a lot while I played the fool.

What came next after I first
stumbled at school but beyond the
reach of others?
Not to be head of my class
but beholden to those others in mass?

"Here in my heart, you get the best of
my love."
Anchored in my life's conformities
—as we pulled into the naked shore—
I pledge to you my spirit, heart, and soul.

I'm surprised I came back easily
from the impotent pictures in my mind.

_____

To determine again what is real,
even remembering I am half blind.

Fresh thoughts were a soothing presence
as I began my laborious task,
like pulling bunny rabbits out of a hat.
Gridlock and happenstance were all I could ask.

All right, it's time to stay indoors;
the elements not distinguished
from weather inhospitable.
Clouds moved east past the ocean's shores.

I continued on beyond the spot
shown by the lighthouse neither close nor far,
from which I could fish for tuna and salmon
in Georges Bank marks the dot.

I fought for a small victory,
a conclusion to adverse events
in the play, the dumb show,
lest the masses of perversity won in their intents.

You showed me, in your ways,
all the truths a man could gain.
So wherever, in what direction I turned,
you'd never lead my hopes
and my love in vain.

I was almost at that point
when I saw the soothsayer
Cassandra at the gates.
"Beware the ides of March,"
so she would relate.

Am I tired of dull, hackneyed ideas?
In what way were my own ideas superior?
I stepped up to the pulpit, the dais,
in the nearby room full of my inferiors.

I will tell the truth as I see it.
I see no great shakes in lying.
"To thyself be true," said Polonius,
a part of a list of desired, axiomatic
phrasing.

I thought we could do it better that way;
women often uploaded my thoughts.
If they respected my intellect,
they deigned not search for macho results
my male cohorts brought.

I slipped on the wet floor of the bistro.
Earlier, I broke a champagne glass.
I was clumsy, with my deficient vision,
but one who never yielded a stone or a
gun against the general mass.

In a half hour, like the one just expired,
the society showed its true colors.
For women as for men,
one's manners had to conform to basic norms.

What news can I make this month
now that Black History Month is over?
If we failed to show public conscience,
what confidence do we have of political cover?

They dragged the truth out of me—
the truth that capitalism is intended to fail.

Even if time is on my side,
fear of socialism will take years to install.

Not having to please my reader
or to compete with fellow poetasters,
I take the long view not to change the world but to install reason
in all boys and girls.

He entertained the scope of the problem:
how to measure, in teacups and teaspoons,
the history of the new millennium affairs
such as in France, ministers and
chargé d'affaires.

I relate to the girl's proposition
to do well in class, not depend on sex.
She was well-endowed physically
but calm as a dove bird in her reflexes.

Gosh, if I continue,
if I go on practically forever,
it's she who allows me to work,
to eat well-mannered with knife and fork.

Where I began an hour ago,
I had no idea what to say.
In a dream world in Sleepy Hollow,
I took whatever license I could follow.

Then comes the hard part,
recording like a typist my inmost thoughts;
I get to the easy part,
exalting my virtues as I did from the start.

What will happen to these leaves?
These barbs of wit called my poetry?

———

Collected like rain from a gutter, never
quite getting far past any mystery.

Clowns in the circus, mascots in
sports
touch my heart gleefully on a dry day
where folks go out to the beach
to watch the fair(er) sex go by.

I knew that musical phrase or turn
when I should know better not to stop.
Would my God or my muse help me
in writing that is hardly slipshod?

Once again, a wave breaks o'er my head.
The sands are clean and beckoning
before I put a toe in or up to my waist.
The danger of the beach leaves without a trace.

As I feel pretty good
in spirit as well as in soul,
tempted by the Greek gods,
birds torn from their nest, sacrificial or odd.

If my spirit moves me
and if I don't worry about the time,
today it's too rainy for the movies
and not at all abandoning
what is rightfully mine.

If I cried for help
from insects around that barrel of waste,
shoo, fly! I hear *buzz, buzz*—
now inactive—and I felt no disgrace.

I must continue on. Time's of the essence.
An elixir, made by a scientist, for a youth
assessing an assault in the world's realities,
with an alcohol level of one hundred proof.

Days of wine and roses
cloy like some Mozart music.
When drunken and high, I escaped
a pattern of imagining—the magic too close.

It all seemed like a dream—
a fantasy—out in the woods,
men without compasses lost
hunting for truffles and mushrooms.

If I go on gallantly,
in a historic time or some phase new,
please forgive my lack of confidence
and what should seem secure and not loose.

She loved to sit and read
beside me at her writer's desk
or sew or read magazines,
designing collages she knew weren't
second best.

An opera diva sang Mozart;
chamber music in a local parlor
couldn't I appreciate the subtler
points
in judging the finer qualities from the start?

The hiker's voice echoed in the mountains.
The poetic refrain heard in Walden Pond,
bellowing like a frog in a bog.

The intrepid listener's
friends gather around.

Once again, I let my feelings show.
How to go on when phrase after phrase
echoed in my ears and mind?
Like Keats and Shelley in words divine.

I can't go on like this for weeks,
for an epoch known for its rabid acts.
I divorce my mind from secondary
reasoning
that in the long run would remain abstract.

To follow King Lear like a fool
upon a three-legged footstool
or before a precipice, a promontory
with Gloucester blind banished so cruel.

In *The Lord of the Flies*, Piggy's
spectacles got broken—
thank God they weren't mine.
What would I have done, in earlier ages,
if I lacked eyesight and was
virtually blind?

Horrors! The battlefield strewn
with nameless corses, lying out in the dust.
Who would bury these nondescript men
when funerals would be held as they must?

In a play, perhaps written by some bard,
where swift actors propelled the context,
I sat in the audience feeling relaxed,
appreciating the actors gesticulating hard.

———

I felt fine as the seasons changed—
cast your seasons to the wind.
All conditions were ripe for compelling
warm days and warm nights until they
did end.

A force of nature compelled me
to go in feverish pace.
Not to worry, standards thrown out
the window
bring successes that I could trace.

I'm doing better than I thought,
dreamed the artist with his oils.
The bright stars and planets
over dull hues did largely prevail.

On this desk, I don't lean too hard,
a scrivener, a master with his paints.
In black and white, the dossier got written,
a methodical method
with his own particular traits.

I'm hearing Bach's baroque music
as if for the first time;
how many centuries ago
did his oratorio music thrive?

He took a deep dive.
Too scared to go on the diving board,
as bikinis circled around him,
his attention, his thoughts were
untoward.

A solitary search sought by evil men
was laid upon his doorstep.

What if his offenses became weak,
leaving no person but himself to
speak?

If, if I seem obscure or scattered
in thoughts vexing, vexatious, and
bold,
my idea of spending all day at the racetrack,
to Hemingway was all the story told.

I was aware at the time
of the colors of the flowers
like Shakespeare's "daisies pied"
I saw the palettes of painters flying.

Once in a while, or whenever
the circus came to town,,
"There's a sucker born every minute,"
said by P. T. Barnum,
he distracted himself with cotton
candy and popcorn.

So fine the way her brown locks
descended nearly to the ground
or down to her waist
in movements swaying,
lovely and in good taste.

In my race against time, I had no fear
that the snows that season would fall;
with nothing to fear but fear itself,
I watched the snowflakes that were
like condensed tears.

The lessons of science interested me;
as for physics, I felt ignorant.

Torque and pressure might define a spaceship—
if we only gave it half a chance.

I took no chances in that époque,
not to settle all my debts—
if someone published
my verse posthumously,
I'd try hard not to have any regrets.

It was so fine just to see you
after so many years;
we hadn't changed at all,
with the charged tunnels of history,
like an engine hammered in our ears.

She held me close;
we hugged and kissed.
If kissing leads to love,
I'd love her until total bliss.

And so the story goes:
She wanted me to set my verse to music.
In art class, she was well occupied.
If I employed effort, my piano might be
prepared to use it.

Recklessly she drove her car,
but she was no hit-and-run driver.
I prevailed on her, earlier that day,
not to rush with the speed of a tiger.

We held on for dear life,
neither of us had any doubt
to conquer the dangers of the city
with the other poor people left out.

If we go no further
on this expedition called life,
would eternity mark us
for thieves in the night?

You brought me good luck
in all intellectual matters of the mind.
So who was I to contemplate
the fallacies that were mine?

Like a train, a locomotive,
tumbling down the tracks,
I reviewed the pace of my progress—
safe bones and muscles intact.

The air was kind to the inhabitants
of Windsor Castle.
It showed to the wind the long history
of the royal family,
pleasant and fair.

I awaited you by the corner
of Twelfth Street and Vine.
Passersby wondering if I were shy,
awaiting for the friendship of that
other guy.

Send a message to Elvis,
a telegram to the Beatles.
Who were these tiny insects
I'd thread through the eye of a needle?

The pretty larks and the butterflies
served as peaceful reminders
of the old days in Penelope's castle,
where even the servants wore blinders.

How is it possible given
you lost so often in poker?
I believe what I saw.
Your losses stung you to the core.

Ah, I shook with the autumn leaves.
Bruised fruit and apples fall onto the ground.
I harvested the low-hanging fruit
in a circle round.

Not processing to be unique or unusual,
whether mostly id or ego,
always looking through a mirror at
myself
or looking glass, opaque and
narrow.

Storybooks, sold to a privileged
reader or to a lonely clerk for the
government,
told a swashbuckling tale of out at sea
where pirates mutinied and the
schooner no longer ran free.

Waiting at the train platform,
I saw a familiar woman who reminded me
of Anna Karenina.
No, it wasn't with any suicidal thoughts,
admiring her carriage through the
railroad carriage.

The color of his skin was black,
like many thought, as of blackest hell.
Brackish red waters swelled
incarnadine

———

at ease around his freedom in winding
circles.

I figure out a puzzle, not a board game.
Music to my ears for my mind to accept.
Where will all men unkind head?
When the waters of oblivion carry you
away or where they led?

Perhaps a poem escaped from my brain—
the setting, a Georgian farm. Slaves chop
cotton.
So how do we have the same slavery
today? Like Emmet Till,
indentured, lynched, lying in the creek
bottom.

"Yes, I'm feeling all right. I write poems."
If, indeed, I seem somewhat pessimistic,
one thing though, what you thought,
I fall into the arms of a mystic.

As I started a new leaf,
a new arrangement, or a new season,
"It's plain. It's crucial to see
how psychology plays tricks on me."

Weary from a ten-mile walk,
I sat me down on a cornerstone,
gathering up my resources.
At present, I felt all alone.

At midnight, the moonlight
played tricks on human eyes.
Down below, the bright afterglow
felt romantic on all sides.

She cared for me, that much I knew;
she proposed to express her love
in unexpected ways—
fresh as the flowers in May in the
morning dew.

It would be so nice to proffer
rewards to the winner.
In that little town where nothing ever happens,
I chose to lay low because of illness.

The army retreated finally,
having not won the whole battle.
As soldiers drank from canteens,
a temporary reprieve from a death
rattle.

They sang in the black church.
A minister's sermon was brief, if pointed.
Church bells rang in the ghetto
where glorious hymns to God were
anointed but not disjointed.

As I tried to rhyme, to relish fresh stanzas,
who came along but that elite critic
throwing cold water on my efforts,
not bending an inch on anything
specific.

I've Got Talent played on the television
where life's fantasies were unloaded.
I questioned not the contrary truth
that resides beneath the church's roof.

"To be or not to be: that is [maybe] the question."
They say I'm unfit, untrue,

two standards like raising a red flag
and not a white one indicating
surrender.

Once started, continued,
in shabby ground that "grows to
seed,"
"Things rank and gross in nature.
Possess it merely."
I'd adapt Hamlet's soliloquy (to my
will or) to my own needs.

I don't seek perfection,
citing I only have so much time
in this life—so toward, so tawdry, and so blind,
I almost have no time to rhyme.

"Quaker oats shot from guns."
That's the only war vocabulary I can stomach.
Lawlessness in America reigns.
Snipers and sharpshooters call
hunting fun.

It so happens I'm chipper today;
my beloved is never far away.
I hunger for human love
or of so much show of demonic
determination that
I can take it in without reprimand.

An author must have something to say—
if not, a clear motif—
like always out of reach
the sparkling sands of the beach.

Do I fear death on such an overcast,
gloomy day?
I'm distracted by the other denizens in
the café.
"Youth lasts forever," I write
in tiny increments. I try ever to make
it right.

Imagine if I felt better, then
I didn't have to worry about earthly ills,
private or public. Derived from pain
whose origin is totally beyond
my view, my ken.

Ah! My restless heart!
I grieved at her going.
Would we be together always
or just to salty tears flowing?

They signaled a speedy retreat
through a broad meadow full of corpses.
It wasn't much of a picnic;
their forces tried to regroup their losses.

What do I mean by that?
I traveled as far as I could go.
In the forest, wild strawberries
and wildflowers
flourish in order like they should.

Shoulder squeeze on down the line.
No other circular order
at home where I'd remain
in the room I rented at the border.

So observe my immediate thoughts—
I wanted to face them in order.
Easy it was to do my task
if I made it to Mexico, south of the border.

In my mind, thoughts disconnected
yet still mesmerized the audience,
like life put in a fantasized trance,
order, and step with a melancholic dance.

As words trickled from my mind,
not confusing me at all,
I wrote sentences into my notebook.
I hoped for striving as I could find.

I listened to an entire concert
in a huge hall with chandeliers.
The walls as high as I've ever seen,
acoustic from side to side did protect.

Their dwelling, their hovel not unusual,
like a clay adobe for native Indians.
I have always wanted shelter
in a domicile in June where we would not swelter.

I reached the end of some sort.
Already I had spit out my wad.
In class where young damsels grew
like sheep, I lacked the ability to play
that sport.

Tired from the disorder of the day.
When sincere solid music
filled my inner void,
I found metal iron late that changes
into steel alloy.

Hurry past the demon to a house
of mirth where I learned to do light
chores in that devil's sympathy—
a symphony where agony and pity
unite.

"Pith and marrow." Don't question Hamlet,
complex mind of many themes.
On that date in April, he mourned
his own mirror image in a rocky,
rickety scene or dream.
I opened the door.
As I turned the key,
a bookcase fell on my head,
like Mr. Bast in *Howards End*.

What I knew, she wanted to know.
Then we two walked down the road.
Side by side like a diamond in the desert,
I found a jewel of a woman but in a world of hurt.

In a peaceful way,
I groomed the flowers.
Sunflowers bought on the street
where no other casual gardeners
could compete.

If Beale Street Could Talk
was a novel by James Baldwin.
Sad Negroes made the Village scene;
fear and the loathing brought them down.

I look no further than myself,
my abilities acquired from my mother,
so the female I lived with now
had no sad traits that I had borrowed.

Knocking on heaven's door,
I asked St. Peter, keeper of the keys.
Better than multiheaded Cerberus,
vain dog at hell's gate, unwilling to
appease or to please.

Down the hill, the lovers sleighed
in the small town of Lenox, Massachusetts.
Snow swept their toboggan along
near Williams College, safely came in
first or last.

As a last resort, a last resource
some poet might have dreamed
or guessed about the riddle of the Sphinx
while I wondered what it all meant.

To be untrue was never my intent.
To her whom I held in the highest esteem,
our affair tossed into the bargain
as a wind rustled through the trees.

What was she so mad about?
I hitched up my pants by the belt,
going to a dusty event;
casually we dressed for the sport.

Like a hurricane, the waves
came crashing—a tsunami.
In panic, the citizens near the coast
were no longer sitting pretty.

I sent a missal to a friend
in homeroom class.
Respectfully she responded;
our flirtation failed fast.

Then the storm came
over the tundra in Russia.
In the steppes of the Urals,
the Caucasus, few dry spots remained.

He used a formula for the baby's bottle.
Near the crib were stuffed animals.
A teddy bear was Jimmy's favorite—
next to whom he loved to cuddle.

The music implied, tenderly,
the tonality in the pianist's heart;
strains of Debussy and of Mozart
enchanted the listeners from the very start.

Waiting for inspiration,
the lions at the gate
behave well with the lion tamer
who, before the circus crowd, felt great.

Why do I work so hard?
Leave stomach for harsh decisions.
A stitch in time saves nine,
why didn't she accept my propositions?

"Felt along the heart," as Wordsworth says
to the matter, the central idea.
Hiking the Lake District,
he'd leave defining philosophy for
another day.

Limited by time and scope,
by the metaphysical in Donne's
philosophy, I tried hard to cope,
study, and not be the only one.

I want to say a few words,
to have something of import to say.
Caught in the rain, I reached for my umbrella—
my better angels, my muse, I'd still revere and pray.

I outdid myself in saying how I felt.
When I went along the shore,
the "multitudinous sea
incarnadine"
did put me in a bind. Always,
the colloquial versus the majestic line
or rhyme.

So far, so good. I was famished with hunger,
desiccated with thirst. Omar Khayyam
nourished me.
Poor orphan, a ward of the state,
restored back to health my awkward
story to relate.

When will I feel pride in what I do?
Under what copies or direction point?
As I was hungry, I had a three-course meal,
deep satisfaction sustained (me) and anoint.

We had a party with all the trimmings—
spin the bottle for those who were eager,
confetti and college flags filled the room,
a supply of apples to dunk was not meager.

Do we have time for one last kiss?
Then lock her in a castle! In London's tower!
So far apart like Pyramus and Thisbe,
never to finalize, to accomplish their
bridal bliss so powered.

I kept watch over the crib.
Chubby and seven ounces, my young boy.
As I felt pride,
I blushed red in the nursery with joy.

What of the classics?
Two epics about Ulysses?
Was it ever too late to sail the Aegean foam?
"The glory that was Greece, the
grandeur that was Rome."

I was in the mood for peace and solace,
for solitary study. Like Wordsworth,
to block out the city's din,
the raucous smell of humanity,
which tawdry era was I in?

After the Fall—what fall?
That of Adam eating the apple
or the complex history of mankind?
Sure, I'd never with sin grapple.

It was all written down in the book
that I never read. Did that mean
I was missing something? Out of love
and grace
or just leaving time for books I wanted
to retrace?

As the gold orb sank in the west,
I marveled at the hordes of ducklings—
a dozen followed their mother,
past yellow daffodils and four-leaf clovers.

Mom started a garden symbolically
filled with impatiens. In the morning sun,
wet with dew, we dug and weeded;
it was really so much fun.

Carry me back to ole Virginia.
and not the Civil War graveyards.
Vast meadows with white crosses
next to cotton fields back home.

We begin with nonviolent protests
in the '60s with astounding hopes
and prayers for the Civil War dead,
who Whitman and Sandburg healed
and fed.

I thought of a typical black man,
a field hand, or Uncle Tom.
With so much patience and persistence,
his road to glory, to paradise was found.

I got myself ready, into gear.
The other sprinters flexed their leg muscles.
I heard the pistol go off.
To win, I'd really have to hustle.

I mused over the Roman Empire, the Pax Romana.
All roads lead to Rome.
Were there tyrants like Caligula or Nero?
Who built the roads? The aqueducts?
Marcus Aurelius and Cicero, who led in
their own manner?

I was certain of the spot as if
the "charts were given" (Emily Dickinson).

With enduring faith, I lead my life.
To hell or paradise, I'll go with my wife.

What was the recipe for success?
Following commands and careful observation.
She was a woman hardy in the kitchen.
The meal a fact, not just a fiction.

I had plenty of time; in love, I was your slave
for decades long. We arrived
at the vital point of not fearing,
seconds ticking along as a flag
that waves.

Tell me why you cried over
insubstantial things
but not crucial decisions. If you ache
for tomorrow,
I will too; through you, I'm validated,
satisfied with meager pains for trying.

The clock was beating against me.
The one on the Congo church knelled
six times.
As dusk, as twilight approached,
shoppers with their groceries at
home arrived.

In a candy store, we bought sweets.
It was, for us, a new adventure.
To but wander beyond the city gates
was also nice as spices from the Far
East left our day's work complete.

I assess my valuables. In need of a new
wallet to hold on my credit cards and dollars
was my Christmas present.
In return, for her
I bought a Madras shirt with a
colored, embroidered collar.

Between a rowboat and a canoe,
I settled for a kayak.
Between a blue Buick and a Chevy,
I chose a Cadillac.
Attach me to the most common choice
that sticks.

If you felt the way I do,
could I save you from the world so onerous?
Two hearts beat as one,
whatever most pleases us.

There are, in life, no easy bargains;
you get what you pay for.
The simplest flower in the sun
gets water at the border's margins.

"So continue," I heard myself say to her.
"Have confidence in your own chosen
speed or direction."
As the rock was too heavy for Sisyphus,
only with strength could he make
allowance or connection.

Finally, the digging and weeding over,
he took pride in watering a rosebush.
When the dog trampled on them
and ate the roses,
he sang, "Red rover, come over."

Where does the truth lie?
Somewhere in the heart.
We have each other, and that's enough.
Chock-full o' nuts at Starbucks gave us
a good start.

Am I resourceful enough?
Can I depend on my own experiences?
She and I, with steady pace,
showed the world we're part of the
human race.

There is no fault on our part.
Of the essentials, we assume the biggest crust.
As we break bread with the wretched,
the homeless tramps raised up from
the dust.

I chose samples, as a traveling salesman,
of encyclopedias and vacuum cleaners.
My footsteps are the work I do
for myself and my clientele.

I choose among choices—in the
material world,
I'm a material witness in and out of
court. Do you want to make a deal?
You offer me a bargain that is really a steal.

Was I in never-never land?
Only one thought at a time, please.
If I wrote more words, would I still be free?
An inner voice dismissed me out of hand.

There is no time left on our journey
past masons and carpenters of all sorts.
So why be troubled by easy stuff
when, at the end of the rainbow, I have
a capable escort?

You tried once to teach me
lessons I already knew—
braves and warriors, chiefs and kings,
all I knew "of a diminished thing"
(Robert Frost).

Toward a pond near a cave,
we did all that a lover of nature required—
my hollowed-out canoe
was my steady bark or tree upright.

"I'm fixing a hole where the rain gets in,"
sang the Beatles in four-part harmony.
Transfixed toward an alien place,
they played their parts with a lopsided
grace and glory.

If you can carry on without me
in this pensive, nightmarish mood,
I'll wake on a day full of chatter
when war kept me absolved.

If I'm wrong in my endeavors
(always to help, to assist you),
I'll try harder. A simple soul,
it's common sense, and no time left
to lose.

I said "Good" to my son on a swing
that I pushed. Other parents around
envied our demure attitude—
a state others felt was profound.

In fits and starts, I began a task
well rooted like a tree.
In an apple orchard, she urged me,
"Take a bite. It'll set you free."

Buckets of rainwater, all right for the animals,
from a faucet, a spigot being of good use,
and I lamented the underrated praise
when farmers drank without any sin
or excuse.

I would do it again if I had to.
Wild notions fit me just fine.
All day, the sun sinks,
enough shadows in the darkness
to fill the kitchen sink.

It matters how I do as I lighten up—
friends gather round in jollity.
I remember not to exploit my role
as a patron in the Deux Maggots café.

It's okay with me as you love me
(will I ever forget that?).
Born to run from birth,
will I ever achieve anything on this
place, this planet called Earth?

When I made a conscious effort
all through a clear day,

like pigs in *Animal Farm* as kings,
"How Orwellian!" said those who
hadn't even read his books,
a poor dishwasher doing a depressing
thing.

I keep starting up like an unbridled horse.
There's no danger in human exercise;
I keep on keeping on as if a pause
would cause me to cease, to
internalize, to cauterize.

As predicted in the news,
the events played out as all suspected.
These days, no misfortune is too great
that evil men would countenance a
travesty like this.

That time I tried in 1962 at Williams
to aggrandize my vocational gems
with women added to my record,
little lovers from Smith I'd retain.

Realizing or reconnecting the extreme
tensions of an hour
when black candidates challenged
their white rivals—
don't go too far downstream,
keep in mind the precious cargo
in the hold further down.

As always, I fought with time.
I well knew I couldn't win.
So I stopped aside to worship at your side—
to regurgitate minutes and hours I
couldn't shun.

Was Emily Dickinson a recluse in
Northampton?
I pictured her a grande dame locally,
writing (I imagined) little nuggets of
gold.
Not sad, she let her semiprivate life
unfold.

I begin again. I employ a better pen.
My words shining in the disinfected sunshine.
A bitter, blowy winter day in Florida,
to rework lines, I don't take any time.

This time, this new pen is too faint.
Oh well, how to reach a happy medium?
People's faces revealed in alien
places
relaxed all the tedium.

I felt that I needed help.
Stop your confused thoughts that linger.
For a long or eternal time in my mind,
I do the work with my brain and my fingers.

Previously, the athlete set the record
for the most hits in a season;
like Malamud's *The Natural*, the ball player
kept his pride and career within reason.

Must I ask her to dance?
Try to find romance Sadie Hawkins–style.
The girls, like the men, stood in line against the wall,
wallflowers who hung there in single file.

Imagine if this well ran dry.
Where would we find fresh water
or oil to propel our cars?
Both resources are vital to human order.

The starving migrants at the border
wish to eat the fruit and grapes they pick;
good politicians feed a hungry child
when provisions didn't arrive in order.

I can't stop loving you,
isn't it clear?
Like the honking of a bus
where a wedding near the Opera
Garnier was near.

I dug deep into my memory.
Seventy-six years of productive thinking
made my life worthwhile, worth living,
along with sufficient sustenance in the
belly.

There were two or more possibilities.
Kristin and I'd prosper like king and queen,
long into the years when time held us close,
the decades together and years in
between.

I was told by the trainer
that for my arthritis,
I needed therapy.
Beyond the pills that sustained me,
where would I pump oxygen readily?

If I bequeath my letters to Kristin,
my oeuvre filling many books,
in the hopes that posthumously, they might be printed,
from endless avalanches, mudslides,
for a bird like a rook.

Without too much excess effort,
I took off time from watching the news,
yet it was me, like Rodin's *The Thinker*
in free fall, free-falling while having the
blues.

I kept it simple.
Outside, spring snuck in;
the lovely lilacs and iris
made me no longer regret the state I was in.

Why write such perfect words?
And to whom do I dedicate
my metaphors and similes of speech
if nobody else seems directly to care?

It was a work of love,
an exercise beyond words,
beyond the borders of the river
Rubicon,
where birds like swans and seagulls
converged.

As a final retort,
in that debate at Tufts,
I felt adequately prepared
from a vague idea to a proposition rough.

What does it matter anyway? Got to start somewhere.
On the western plain, living things are meager.
I've got enough sense to accept the
desert sands
as Mount Rushmore appears like the
grand scope of man.

How do I feel? The critic asked.
I gave him little to work with.
A secretary wondered what I do in
preparing for a biographical
interview.

Up to schedule, he had to meet some
special queries
that others might take in asking him
questions
about the fact of death,
grief, angst, poverty; he would have
to face life's shadows
like the hard, cold trailing of a hearse.
It made the horse's traces worse.

I didn't do too well at the hour of our Lord.
The idea of praying in the church
or cathedral in a modern city
left me cold, salvation found
elsewhere.

I studied the map of Paris, divided into
arrondissements.
Three major structures: the Eiffel Tower, Notre
Dame, and the Sacré-Cœur.
I felt warm in my heart,
trekking in tandem with other sightseers
whose thinking was not far apart.

Along the Great Wall of China,
the answer came to life—
of Asian Buddhas and Siamese twins,
on the diet that kept them thin.

Henceforth, I'll be more objective
(as if objectivity would pertain).
From tyrants to philosopher-kings,
Plato quoted Socrates for the synthesis
he made of things.

Free to be silent, to find enjoyment,
whether in music, art, or Shakespeare.
I listen to the television in the
next room,
fearing as I learn of misfortunes
spoken.

Left alone to not overstudy—
with music, art, and pastimes
available—
the teacher toward his kids
would never lead them down a course forbid.

A mishap in London, on the left side of the road,
medics hurried as paralegals joined
in broad daylight the old man who drove
his roadster right into the "elm tree
bole" (Robert Browning).

Yes, you fooled me. Was it fair
to gamble my life savings away?
My 401(k) dwindling to the size of a
raisin.
Depend not on getting rich

someday.
No. I wasn't caught unawares.

You mistake me when you think I write
paperback potboilers
with the wit of a meat grocer
or fishmonger with a pearl earring
leading us astray as I lose my writer's
bearing.

"Lay on, Macduff, and damned be he
who first cries 'Hold enough!'"
Anxiety in the castle, the queen sleepwalking
gave clues of great moment intruding.

Have you no pride, Esther Primm,
with a scarlet letter? You aren't a
witch or part of a witch hunt,
unfairly challenged like a Jew in the
diaspora.

What they're discussing is bad.
Do my ears hear part of a witch
hunt?
Who's chosen now? A charlatan innocent
of a century's probe, not willing to
pay the rent?

What was at the core of that forbidden fruit?
Speakers whisper in the anteroom.
With hopes that would sink the Titanic,
pundits and politicos weigh their
ideas, all in a panic.

There's no rush. I'm tolerant
of others' political views. After all,
there's peril in the southern mistral.
Even sailors must be aware of not
walking the plank.
Fool me once, shame on me. Fool me
twice, shame on you.

We'll reverse the order of the seasons.
Even Van Gogh found colors *éblouissant;*
they gathered in a glittering
summation that defied anyone's vision
or wisdom.

You released me of my obligations.
Until I fell into Bunyan's Slough of
Despond.
Three great poets—Thomas Gray,
Hardy, and Milton—
taught us in our criticisms to prudently
respond.

What is the riddle of the pyramids,
the Sphinx?
Who "cleft the devil's foot"
(Ben Jonson)?
I measure each step in the Great Wall of China,
except "something there is that doesn't
love a wall"!
That defies that well-thought idea complex.

Don't fail by forgetting a thought.
Realize they may mean much to others.
When my lover returns from God
knows where,
I breathe free, my exploits returning,
registering as they ought.

———

I'm always constricted by time.
Wiser would it be for me to avoid
the impossible.
"Uncle Sam covers my bets,"
yet I forge to the front with no regrets.

Start again? I've barely begun—
following the strictures of my soul—
but all this ended at the
caveman prehistoric or Neanderthal
in one roll.

What you wanted, I got it for you,
even though I couldn't ever give you energy.
The drama like in *The Winter's Tale*,
we applaud that comedy that could
have been a dirge.

I imagine a lot after that lofty movie.
Willem Dafoe playing Vincent van Gogh,
and what else have I learned today?
Besides a Pandora's box of emotions
that left me more insecure
than a tugboat in a fog.

I answer with regret how I feel
after you followed my career in reverse.
No, I don't mix metaphors
unless you'll think they're all rehearsed.

Once again, you ask what my aim is.
The question again presents itself
like water off a duck's back.
I swiftly think I'm in a waterfall that
other writers lack.

No, regardless of the music playing
and the song and dance it conveys,
I do it my own way—a musical prodigy?
Mandolins and lutes in Shakespeare's day.

You make it seem so easy.
Cinnamon girl, cowgirl in the sand,
why do I love thee better than all the rest?
Oh, don't doubt how fervently I am blessed.

That time tired, in the dark evening,
when the thrush and wren take their rest,
the nocturnal owl hoots.
It's the time for me to take everything
that you give.

"Help!" the Beatles cried.
Their humanity not lost on any others,
musical dreams and mortal thoughts,
as me and my lady do what is implied!

Intuition that is ironic suits me just fine.
I'm not doing other's dirty work or labors;
I tell it the way I see it
without falling out of the queen's favor.

Who are the characters, demons, and shadows
of my darkling night? Must I steadily
approach where my soul meets my spirit?
No, none of this phantasmagoria is allowed.

Do I wish to "pack it in, take it down to LA?"
I'll leave you, baby, tonight in the event
some folk singers lull us to sleep
if I don't forget, like Robert Frost,

that "I have promises to keep,
And miles to go before I sleep,
And miles to go before I sleep."

Am I forgetful of my obligations?
The needs of my mate in the next
room?
Unless I realize how duty and fun
unite
like Edgar Allen Poe, forget us in the
gloom.

Finish up, I think, to my favorite songs;
let these poems join the others.
I'm skillful tonight. In the heavy
darkness,
like a wall of mirrors,
I neglect to show my weaknesses.

"How sweet it is," added James Taylor,
"to be loved by you." Always rock solid,
I take my task perhaps too seriously.
There is beauty in the world if only
untoward.

I imagine things too serious or too
unwieldy.
Others praise my use of words.
If I can manage simple things—
allegories or metaphors—
like my abilities, I admire her carriage,
her courage.

Le mot juste. I mention it once again.
Obey rhythm, like a bird's or wind's

call;
the hoot of an owl, nocturnally;
the mouth of the thrush, naturally.

Beware. Of what? False prophets?
Russian icons? After years of practicing versification,
it shouldn't take too much effort—
better than being a secretary in charge
of public relations.

What can I say next to appease your soul?
To retain your temper, your traits?
With fear and loathing, I approach you
to suggest a vacation in Las Vegas.

What do I want for you in the eons
of history ahead? Only to be with you
while seas flow and mountains descend,
like breasts with spilled milk long gone.

You asked me why I am limited
in scope and art like a man disgraced.
Confronted, you ask? With reams of material
by myself, I will address these
challenges in a setting immaterial.

Danger: Work Ahead. Cones divided the new road.
Our Chevy bowled down the way—
like a robot machine out of gas
or an orange piston running too fast.

"I tried," they said. At least they made the effort.
Before the tide rushes in, ebbs and flows,
let's take the field of muddy earth—
a garden, where people go, won over
with mirth.

Ripley's *Believe It or Not*,
there were no facts that really
impressed me.
I drove at sixty miles per hour.
I was a master of ceremonies, not a jester.

At the end of the drama,
a deus ex machina tidied up all the details.
Was it too forced an ending?
Hamlet wrestling in Ophelia's grave
with Laertes, histories changing.

Lullaby and good night.
So starts another day.
How come I dream always of you
when the furry clouds part their
pillowy hopes away?

I am an entity only consumed by thought,
of all the homebodies who pray, who dream.
I'm an integer, a digit. By God,
I'd get beyond myself if you, too, were
what you seem.

I have a mistress, like the Dark Lady of
the Sonnets.
Restless nights lead to hectic days.
I made a deal with the devil—fearless;
I won the prize—your eternal caress.

Something happened today.
Standing by the bloody Tower,
I penned words
to a variety of poetasters—
a challenge rich in the fatal history of
Richard III.

As you see, I've wasted lots of time,
time that I don't have much control of
or much of.
In Monet's gardens,
tender tendrils clinging in their prime.

Just thinking about you.
I got a letter in the mail.
What absence, like Rimbaud:
"Quelle saisons, quelle chateaux,
mon ame est sans defaut?"

The finale, like at the start,
felt like the explosion of a cannonball.
When anger or anxiety swept over me,
I resorted to classical music or art.

She looked so fine.
She called me a cool dude.
Decades divided us,
commended our tryst not to be crude.

Just got to let you know,
my love may not stand out as much as the next guy.
So what means can I use?
Succulent plants and cacti planted where
rocks and stones just stood by.

Where did it all begin?
According to Wordsworth, at birth.
He and Coleridge were soul mates,
expressing themselves with ever-
present pleasure and mirth.

I give praise to the fruits of the earth:
flowery backgrounds in which they thrive,
with humans marching along down the hedgerows.
Hawthorn and clematis on the turf.

I decided to leave the juicy parts until later,
knowing it takes time to warm up.
If only I could catch my stride,
like a butterfly winging with singular pride.

As I jump from one book to another,
compounding knowledge like a fast train,
I felt my body and brain tell me something:
assimilation in
free thought not a bother.

I succeeded in that athletic event,
discus or javelin like the ancient Greeks
who competed in Attic strife.
Hardy bodies, hermaphrodites
provided sexual relief.

I wasn't sure of myself,
yet the phrases of lyrics came naturally,
threatening no deadline, unlimited,
no feature I couldn't add factually.

To succeed in certain goals
in an empty cafeteria,
I made a play for that outspoken waitress
whose tenor and physicality I so admired.

I willed it all to her.
Would I see her beyond the grave?
In a home cemetery beside our house,
I was interred under a Star of David.

If ever I should leave you,
it wouldn't be in springtime.
Seasons change but the energy remains.
We feel the sweet sustenance of
cowslips and violets in the rain.

I ride along while others speed.
Legs churning on their racing bikes,
what a pretty picture! Admiring the countryside
in the Tour de France, they took the
lead.

At least I tried. Approached nearby
obstacles,
I didn't seek for originality.
I was wasted in the dust.
Lest clients wanted more, I trust.

God help us. I pray for solace.
But no voice answers.
Between old and young,
my pants are held up by suspenders.

Beauty like a male peacock raises his fan.
I pluck feathers to wear in my cap.
As I walked through the county fair,
admirers think of fowl stuffing there.

If I turn to you, girl (and if you are always there),
the sun descends in degrees.
We have no expectation of a moon.
We have it all, all the love we share.

At least I made an effort
in that café, restaurant, or bistro.

We dined like kings in a brasserie,
like peasants or jesters, not like heroes.

Just as well, let imagination invade
like a fox in a chicken coop or henhouse.
I expect something to be done,
a flash of lightning and thunder.

May my hands always be busy
and not destructive—that's God's asserted law.
One's fist is just as good as another.
To be less a stranger,
first, be a brother.

It's true, this political season,
that democracy goes on trial.
We are at a crossroads,
like Johnny Tremain, delivering the
Boston Post Road's mail.

That is where it all began,
where patriots threw the tea in the
Boston Harbor.
Puritans and pilgrims,
we have much to defend, to feel proud of.

Does the future go on until eternity?
Rabbis and emirs attest to knowing the answers;
only Shakespeare and few men would declare
the truth beyond the common fare.

Will I never quit this joyous bantering?
Apply my feather to ancient parchment?
If given time, I'll claim to apply—
to rest only when my ink runs dry.

Another beginning, yesterday was such a sunny day,
ordered and charted almost without notice.
I should rest while Kristin dozes,
only Keats and Wordsworth also,
hiding their love behind tulips,
violets, and roses.

We came down a frozen, frosty path
with nothing new at that particular moment.
Go beyond the region to immortals'
terrain,
only bound by the endless marvels of
Paradise Lost.

I sympathize fully with your weakness.
In certain social situations, when I, too, start to tumble down
a well with murky water
and I feel like a hero defeating his own disaster.

Yes, I went too far, only faintly thinking
what the end of my journey might be,
to penetrate a hole in the enemy
lines
rather than be lynched, hang from a tree.

Bob Dylan's poetry and philosophic wit
was more than ever I hoped for.
I forgot the subject, but little mattered
in matters of living: peace and war.

I have time to wait, to study real things
as steady as an oak.
If I'm buried by a yew tree,
I'd be more than happy to share the
sod of common folk.

There once was a lady from London
who sailed to Ireland on a muffin.
All around they hailed her elevated state,
munching on marmalade, tea, and cake.

Mama, you've been on my mind.
From pole to pole,
like Eskimos we kiss,
pale penguins forever, progress.

Once I began, it was easier
than a Hail Mary pass.
Little fear of missing a catch,
mackerel and eels in the water like glass.

And yet and yet again,
they move the goalposts.
Block and tackle like in fishing,
I made a catch, a touchdown, alas!

Often in Paris it comes to mind,
a place where citizens react to the weather.
Why in the rain do they all have black umbrellas?
Like Caillebotte ever extending their tether.

A cowboy on the outlaw trail
where even cactus isn't at all special,
he wrestled steers for a living,
for his cowgirl he wouldn't fail.

Since I feel fine, girl, why do you feel helpless?
Is someone or something on your mind?
And I know you well, your every mood;
so please follow me down the line
and don't fall behind.

She had more senses than me.
(No, I don't refer to common sense.)
Olfactory, she breathed sweeter air,
so, too, colors in small doses.
Her five senses caught me unawares.

Michael, row the boat ashore. Hallelujah.
The river Jordan is chilly and cold.
Hallelujah.
Chills the body but not the soul.
(Lessons I should learn before I get too old.)

What next? Van Gogh thought to himself.
In another self-portrait, his spirit died.
So he cut off his ear to please
a prostitute with many a sigh.

I bought bulgy art books sold cheap.
I couldn't resist their purchase.
Painters young and old
who told
their stories in glorious pigments gold.

I used a pen so scratchy.
Who would know the difference?
A large space between work and utility,
no measurements filled my pages.
Would my poems survive the ages?

I do what I can in these expiring hours.
Don't allow the perfect be the enemy of the good!
In difficult foreign courses,
I do not diminish those who play the fool.

I would think before I spoke.
Where did the ideas, the impulses come from?
"Gather ye rosebuds while ye may."
I'd singularly strive before heaven's door.

Rich flowers—peonies and petunias—
overgrew the garden path.
Relax. I smelled this wonderland of pansies
on all their faces distorted but sure in craft.

Ask me again where I've been,
and I'll tell you in no uncertain
terms.
Self-praise wasn't a pearl of self-flattery.
The road not fatiguing, not faltering
until the end.

Sing a song for me. Rock me to sleep.
Ancient kings and prophets in a great hall
spoke to me in undertones
weak and lowly, but lovely,
left me standing ten feet tall.

Can I go on like this?
While consuming Wordsworth's
The Prelude,
my concentration acting secure
beyond the bounds of comprehension
never rude or crude.

I was too abstract. The lines on the canvas showed their pigments
on the palette
form slowly, appeared as if from
outer space, devoted from zero
to soulful granite.

I'd create, in materials, something out of nothing.
Can you challenge me further?
Nothing from nothing leaves nothing;
must I be a fortune-teller or a soothsayer?

The actors were strained in tensile strength.
We left the movie more stunned than at the start.
Fight on, I thought like a boxer,
a knockout at last report.

The kids saw rats.
It wasn't the healthiest of environments.
Shaken to the roots, the parents
besieged the landlord to mention the
event.

Sadly interrupted, I change the subject.
It must have been my fault.
I would rest with complaints today
that made it easier to justify a faulty report.

What things you needed, I got for you.
"Rough-hew them how you may."
I needed relief before the sands of
time's hourglass
judged me either way
before death's decree.

I worked and reworked the project in my mind.
I filtered out impurities and defects
what had been in dollars and cents,
allowing politics to take a back seat
that I could preserve in my defense.

It touched me to the core.
The heart of the matter.
Were you and I victims
of the slow rain's patter?

I can do it, I thought confidently.
Though thieves and pickpockets in the
Paris Metro
troubled my soul, but less than
the dire woes according to the lack of petrol.

Tell me why the stars do shine;
I forgot them in my nocturnal walk
past stiles and lampposts in the dark
and parking meters where you had to
pay a fine.

In compensation, my weak eyes
gloried in or glorified great art;
it fixed, it fixated my mind
where my vision would usually show
its drawbacks apart.

Did I have things to do?
Additions to my latest book—
easy it was to add on new paragraphs—
like hurt ladies that time forsook.

Hush, little baby, don't you cry.
I wouldn't wish to be in your shoes.
Text follows or flows more easily
from ancient tales not yet gratified
or in the groove.

I wouldn't go down in history as one
who defied truth, like Whitey the Teflon Don.
With no compunction, not set in time,
the gods in heaven thereby would
surely have fun.

Here comes the judge.
We still live in a fascist police state.
"Blue lives matter," sang the cops
who, with cudgel and long gun,
would overcome many a one.

I delay my duties. Sweltering in December,
I put off *mes devoirs*.
In what respect, I asked myself,
the heat defied me all the more?

Limited by time and scope,
by the metaphysical in Donne's poems,
a world of hurt opened for me
where I fabricated my challenge all alone.

Don't tear the fabric of our dreams.
The thief was caught in whole cloth
by the spinning wheel. Girls sewed rugs.
In a factory they slaved
up the to the roof beams.

Following the circle's diameter,
he did the math; the sums wouldn't add up.
He wrote equations in the sand.
Archimedes's solutions would forever stand.

I'd query what is the question—
it's not "to be or not to be."

Suicide not at all mentioned in
Shakespeare,
its all-too-human characters merit
honorable mention.

In the modern idiom, bad actors fill the stage,
dad hombres like Don Quixote.
I risk forgetting the clumsy ones,
like Polonius or Touchstone, once all the rage.

On a downhill vector, I skied the mountain.
Avoid the moguls, I recalled.
Ice defied the northern slope,
the sun blinding their eyes.

It was a shame
he couldn't control his instincts.
For better or worse, he pledged
not to be dirty or raise a stink.

You can do better.
You can do worse.
In Dublin town, they dreamed of green fields,
the color on a lawn and a country scene.

Is she going to give me more time?
I'm tired from too much headwork.
An Indian headdress in a museum
with the ferocity of a Turk.

"I look around me,
and I see it isn't so."
The word *love* in the English language,
couples unaware, "shoot the moon"
"in spades" in a felicitous mood.

Hold that line.
The football players downfield
in force, in a tug-of-war.
One really hard effort made would be fine or real.

Don't be sinful;
watch your ways.
Let the sunshine in
to brighten all your days.

She didn't like to read.
She had other things to do.
Formally and assuredly,
wisdom came into view.

I'm unsuccessful so far.
So why go on?
If only happenstance and luck
would hurry, give me fruit to pluck.

That would be simple enough.
I have the whole rest of the day.
Perform miracles, willy-nilly,
try new chords on the piano I play.

As usual, she allowed me a wide berth.
Always I could count on her permission to work.
The screen, the curtain drawn,
not letting customers room to go berserk.

Their conversation seemed to idle;
no one used the time allowed.
What I saw a result of overhearing
the discussion moot but proud.

"I'll try to follow in your footsteps,"
I said to the medicine man.
Folk back home would wonder
about the folksy magic again.

It was an abortive attempt—
unsubstantiated in time.
What seemed worthwhile
was but an illusion, a failure to rhyme.

I struggled on against the grain.
I chopped wood for winter's fire.
Today it would be different
if I'm allowed revision without blame.

I tried—Lord alone knows how—
to meet my New Year's resolutions.
Many opportunities to beat the band
as in Times Square, like going to a
Broadway show.

I've sought clarity of expression.
I have a hard time mounting the stairs
to not slip on the carpet, the steps.
I must stay at all times fully
aware.

Unaware, the soldiers stood in line
to take a glance at the map
of Iraq and nearby Iran,
Shiite and Sunni since time began.

Wary of feeling hopeless
by the fun stalls at a county fair;
couples listened to the barkers shout
their persuasions to buy their wares.

My effort was terrible,
sad to say.
Sorry for what I attempted
on such a lovely sunny day.

The child nearly fell down the well.
It was no made-up story.
To avoid the rain, the crew
supported the efforts propped up by the
power and the glory.

Not satisfied with her efforts,
she took a long time with her makeup.
On the stage, she would try hard
to have a success, have a good report.

Of all his successes, the one he treasured most
was to profit from the time
well done above all else
rather than linger long standing in line.

The failure of his effort loomed large
in the overall collection of his merits.
With no time to waste, to wait,
he'd persist long and to his credit.

In court, he argued for his client.
Would the latter be judged guilty
Or innocent in the eyes of the law—
was it the luck of the draw?

Feeling sober enough to go to work
and not lacking the patience needed
to dig up the earth, his task
lasted a whole time without rest.

Once in days of wine and roses,
I struggled with the alcohol's dregs.
Farther apart, the disease left me
sober but tempted by a keg.

I abided by regulations
yet disgusted with the signs
of Keep Out and Beware: Danger.
I paused before again, feeling resigned.

Still I kept on competing,
God knows how hard I tried.
In a sport using sweat and tears,
removing my T-shirt, all other efforts
denied.

I headed for the hills.
Every day another project.
I see a vision where once there was none,
groves and orchards yellow with sun.

If I may appear jealous
and I stick up for myself
in what is right, my love
may put me in a rung above.

I take a deep breath,
returning tit for tat.
Nothing illegal, no,
I'd love to have you and that's that.

If I may, please allow me
the courtesy of asking you to dance.
Did the fox trot slowly
in what looked like spirited romance?

Then again and again, I can wait.
The minute intervals of Father Time.
I alone persevered against the shot clock,
employing all means to predict good luck.

Why I ignored her, I don't know.
I moved with speed among the hazards.
Nowhere to be found, I used my instinct
to glean the wheat crop as the storm gathered.

Was I "still crazy after all these years"?
You must admit it was a labor of love.
I appealed to Jesus, my judge,
to certify my sanity from God the Father
above.

You can't say I never sought
your attention, your loving glance.
As a bowler, I achieved a perfect game;
as a knight or wight, with a shield and a
lance.

A state trooper with civil intentions
survived a long career of service.
His wife and kids protected,
there was some disappointment under
the surface.

"Janie's Got a Gun," a tune by Aerosmith.
Like the Stones, a booming wall of sound.
How did I get misled off course by this?
In my brain and ears, the rhythm pounds.

Shadowboxing, the greatest sparred
with another heavyweight from the hood;

whence they came, no one knew,
at least not injured as they feared.

"He's got the whole world in his hands."
The choir led the congregants in song.
The sad pianist dreamed of being elsewhere.
Meanwhile, his fingers did no wrong.

Tell me why I pined over you.
I perceived a runaway train.
It clung tightly to the railroad ties
from Boston to Providence and back again.

I saw her face in the moonlight.
Her blond locks rich and lovely.
When she turned her head, her profile
I considered; I compared to other
ladies profusely.

I wasn't afraid to go on.
Like a steamer, I plowed through
brackish water
or of frigates out of what war or battle
when sailors feared a stone in their
saddle.

What sins were avoided
in the Indian's rain dance?
As they rose with the sun,
not a gun but an archer in a game of
chance.

So sorry, so sad, the things in our times
we would rather forget about
than "those fears we know not of,"

"a bourn from which no traveler returns"—
a collation of famous lines.

With the wind at my back,
I bound through Wordworth's Lake
District like a roe.
Hills and mountains alongside,
the echoes redound on walls ruddy and black.

How easily the snake slithers
and slides in the grass.
Satan disguised bodes no good,
evil to Adam and Eve delivered.

"The best" have urgent "intensity," says Auden,
in league with fellow poet William B. Yeats.
They well praised the years even of Ireland,
not lost but of settled conflict speak.

And so I followed along another day
where winter winds caused wolves
to howl;
all of nature is good and maternal
when affecting fairly dogs both mangy and gray.

The rain in torrents stunned the land,
soaked the very clothes and socks.
No one henceforth would be spared,
except whether monkey, horse, or fox.

"I beg your pardon. I never promised you a rose garden."
Where the flowers grow, there go I
where birds and bees connected the network
through the green lawn overseen by a
gardener.

I began at the beginning where I saw
success starting to be achieved.
Our country cleared up its act,
fulfilled the high hope they received.

Lycidas "shook his mantle blue.
Tomorrow to fresh fields and pastures new."
It was the death of a fellow poet
Milton had in mind,
not just symbolic but imitative in kind.

Pictured myself in a tropical paradise
in Tahiti or Bora Bora;
do people truly visit these
isles?
The summer lasts all year long
when the waves break single file.

CPSIA information can be obtained
at www.ICGtesting.com
Printed in the USA
BVHW081933170619
551233BV00002B/7/P